INKLINGS

Cartoons and Caricatures by Bruce MacKinnon

Introduction by Jim Meek

NIMBUS PUBLISHING

Nimbus Publishing Limited
P.O. Box 9301, Station A
Halifax, Nova Scotia
B3K 5N5

Design: Steven Slipp, GDA, Halifax
Cover illustration: Bruce MacKinnon
Printed and bound in Canada by Gagné Ltée

Canadian Cataloguing in Publication Data

MacKinnon, Bruce
Inklings, cartoons and caricatures
ISBN 0-921054-53-X
1. Canadian wit and humour, pictorial. I. Title.
NC1449.M32A4 1990   320'.0207   C90-097594-6

To someone with a real sense of humour—the woman who married me.

Acknowledgments

Bob Chambers, for being a friend and an inspiration; G.W. Dennis, for making it all possible; Ken Foran and Jane Purves, for letting me get my foot in the door; Jim Meek, Dean Jobb, and Bretton Loney, for being my guffaw meters and part-time news analysts; Reid MacLean, the nicest lunatic I know; Arthur and Peter Moreira, for their respective contributions to this book; Bob Howse, for patience, tolerance, and the Joe Howe concept; Mom and Dad, for all the charcoal pencils and sketchbooks; Toni and Buck, for the phone calls and support; Aunt Chris, for encouraging me to read *Mad;* the South End Day Care, for being there for me and thousands of other working parents.

Contents

Introduction

By Jim Meek
Senior editorial writer and columnist
for the Halifax *Chronicle-Herald* and
Mail-Star

Like all good cartoonists, Bruce MacKinnon is a public resource. When he gets sick or goes on holiday, Nova Scotians take it personally. If readers turn to the editorial page of the province's largest daily newspaper and find no MacKinnon cartoon, they mope around all day, as if their dog had died during the night.

Why?

MacKinnon tackles the issues of the day in a manner that is always insightful but never predictable. When Premier John Buchanan suggested in the spring of 1990 that the province might join the United States if Québec separated, political opponents called him a traitor, and editorial writers became apoplectic. MacKinnon, on the other hand, didn't get angry: he got even. He dressed Buchanan as Uncle Sam in a parody of the famous American recruiting poster "Uncle Sam wants you." The emperor was shown to have no clothes. (In fact, MacKinnon has stripped Buchanan bare so often that no one would blink an eye if the premier were spotted walking naked down the main street of Halifax whistling "Dixie.")

As the "Uncle John" creation demonstrates, cartoonists such as MacKinnon get to the heart of the matter without wasting words. They transform the instinctive wisdom of common people into something funny and, at times, into something profound. Is there a keener insight into the character of the late Harold Ballard—the curmudgeon who transformed the Toronto Maple Leafs into a national joke—than the one MacKinnon provides? A lawyer reading from Ballard's will, in a cartoon published before the details were made public, says it all: "He took it with him." Of course, Ballard didn't actually take it with him: cartoonists are interpreters, not reporters; seers, not historians.

And being prophets, they get away with much more than journalists, who deal in mere words. After MacKinnon started working for the Halifax Herald newspapers, in 1985, I soon learned that pictures have visceral appeal and primal staying power. By the time he began producing one cartoon a week, I had been working for

The Chronicle-Herald and *The Mail-Star* for the best part of a decade, trying to make sense of fish, oil, politicians, and other foul-smelling commodities. Important stuff—or so I thought.

But no one cared. All Haligonians wanted to talk about was the new cartoonist, the guy with the red ponytail sprouting improbably out of the back of a head so bald that it risked caricature as a billiard ball. The Herald listened to popular opinion and hired MacKinnon full time in 1986, before someone else made him an offer he couldn't refuse. The newspapers had finally found a worthy successor to Bob Chambers, the beloved cartoonist who retired in 1977 with two National Newspaper awards to his credit. (MacKinnon himself has won three Atlantic Journalism awards in a row, and it's only a matter of time before the rest of the country discovers him.)

MacKinnon was only a 16-year-old high-school kid when Chambers put away his brushes. Born in 1961, MacKinnon grew up in Antigonish—the home of St. Francis Xavier University, where Brian Mulroney was a student and Allan MacEachen was a teacher. (MacKinnon managed to escape both these influences and still does.) The budding artist made his way through school, played sports (hockey), and went to church. At 14, he started drawing a cartoon for the local weekly, the most improbably named newspaper in the English-speaking world, *The Casket*. Then, drawing was just a hobby. In fact, MacKinnon claims that the approval of his peers and the discipline of a deadline, not the muses of inspiration, drove him to improve his skills.

It was his later restlessness that really schooled him in the cartoonist's art. By his own reckoning, he has worked at between 40 and 50 jobs. He hauled lobster traps from the choppy seas off Nova Scotia, took the well-travelled journey "down the road" to Alberta, to work on the rigs, cleaned parking lots, mopped up slop in a college cafeteria, worked as a shopping-mall portrait artist, performed for one day as a street musician, and played guitar and sang for two nights at the Orient Lounge in Antigonish. His toughest yet most rewarding job was caring for his daughter, Robyn, while his wife, Peggy, continued working in "the real world." (He and Peggy have since had a second child, Jamieson, and now, it is her turn to work at home.)

Somewhere along the way, MacKinnon developed street sense, which the legendary Aislin of *The Gazette* has defined as an understanding of the "frustrations of the average individual in dealing with suspicious factors that exert control over our lives." Street smarts on their own, however, do not a cartoonist make—let alone a draftsman and caricaturist of the first rank. MacKinnon's academic training was nearly as varied as his career: a year in arts at St. Francis Xavier University; a stint in fine arts at Mount Allison University, in Sackville, New Brunswick; and then a move to the Nova Scotia College of Art and Design, in Halifax. (NSCAD is largely ignored by the denizens of this old seaport town but is described by its devotees in that vague and parochial phrase "world class.")

By the time MacKinnon knocked at the Herald's door, he had it all: talent, training, and street smarts. He also had the most important weapon in any cartoonist's arsenal: the ability to see those with power, money, and privilege from the point of view of those who have less or none of the above. Like most "ordinary Canadians"—to steal a banal phrase from the New Democrats—he instinctively turns a skeptical and suspicious eye to those politicians and businessmen who seem to have an inordinate amount of control over our lives, our national agenda, and our pocketbooks. He has what reporters call a "good bull detector." To put it more elegantly, he does a credible job of "afflicting the comfortable and comforting the afflicted."

And when the occasion arises, MacKinnon proves himself a cartoonist of the highest order. He possesses that rare ability to say just the right thing at just the right time and in just the right way, and it leaves an indelible impression on his audience. One example makes the point. It's late November 1988. The Conservatives under Brian Mulroney are back in power. Free trade with the United

States is as imminent as Monday morning. And even the staunchest proponents of reciprocity are a little jittery about consummating a trade deal that is a repudiation of so much of Canadian history.

Enter MacKinnon.

He depicts Canada as a frightened woman who has awakened from a bad dream. Sitting next to her in bed is a lecherous Uncle Sam, smoking a triumphant cigarette and leering malevolently at his latest conquest. "Ouaaaaagh!" fair Canada screeches when she recognizes Uncle Sam. And thus, MacKinnon pictorially posed the question that few journalists would put into words and that fewer newspaper publishers would print: Did we just get screwed? The cartoon is as lasting as the one Aislin drew of René Lévesque after the late premier had led the Parti Québécois to power in 1976. In that cartoon, Lévesque utters one small piece of advice: "O.K. Everybody take a valium."

This is cartooning as high art. Millions of words were published on free trade, some by writers as formidable as Mordecai Richler and Robertson Davies. Most Canadians cannot quote one sentence from all that output, gem or dross. Once seen, however, MacKinnon's cartoon is not forgotten.

Current events in Nova Scotia haven't hurt MacKinnon, either. Since he started at the Herald, the province's political life has unfolded like something concocted by the witches in *Macbeth*. One cabinet minister was booted out of the Tory caucus, and later the Legislative Assembly, for cheating on his expense accounts, but not before Premier John Buchanan shed a few tears in the legislature. The justice system has been under assault ever since it became known that Donald Marshall, Jr., a Micmac Indian, spent 11 years in jail for a murder he didn't commit. One judge was unceremoniously dumped from the bench because he lectured battered women on the need to obey their husbands and cited scripture in defence of his views. The premier, meanwhile, set the tone of one session by barking at Liberal leader Vince MacLean. (Yes, that's barking, as in *woof, woof*.) And so it goes. Nova Scotia hasn't exactly been a model democracy, but it's a joy for journalists, and the resulting brouhaha has transformed provincial politics into national news.

What else can be said about MacKinnon? That he likes basketball and Gretzky.

That he is a Canadian cartoonist by theme. His predecessors in this century, not to mention the last one, also produced a lot of work on the unholy trinity of national politics—trade with the United States, language policy, and the Constitution. John Bengough, the best-known Canadian cartoonist of the last century, for example, published a work in 1879 that was reproduced in *The Hecklers*. In it, Mademoiselle Québec tells Sir John A. Macdonald to "mind his own federal business, and permit us to manage our local affairs to suit ourselves." *Plus ça change …*

MacKinnon also works within a Canadian tradition of caricature. American cartoonists draw public figures with tiny heads and huge bodies. There is already a standard George Bush caricature south of the border. Canadian caricaturists, like MacKinnon, tend to forge their own way and put huge heads on small bodies.

Variety and versatility are hallmarks of MacKinnon's work as well. He covers a wide range of territory, as this book illustrates. His caricature of Don Cherry trying to climb out of his shirt collar and the cartoon featuring Margaret Thatcher and Nelson Mandela are every bit as effective as cartoons featuring Mulroney or Buchanan.

In the end, all readers need to know is that MacKinnon is provocative, compelling, and talented. Like Aislin and Duncan Macpherson, he has the stuff of which publishers' dreams—and nightmares—are made.

Mugshots

2

Don Blenkarn

David Suzuki

Robert Bourassa

Peter Gzowski

Wayne Gretzky

Don Cherry

Michael Dukakis
"Only two things come from Massachusetts,
lobsters and liberals."—George F. Will

Margaret Thatcher

Ayatollah Khomeini

9   Nelson Mandela

THE
SATANIC VERSES

Salman Rushdie

Ronald and Nancy Reagan

I <u>AM</u> OLD ENOUGH
TO BE PRESIDENT..!
I <u>AM</u> A
<u>GROWN</u> UP..!
I AM I AM I AM!!

Dan Quayle

Provincial

Family court judge Raymond Bartlett is criticized for verbal abuse of women in the courtroom, preaching subservience and quoting the Bible in his decisions.

A series of scandals at Province House is highlighted by the conviction of cabinet minister Billy Joe MacLean for cheating on his expense accounts.

THE BUCHANAN
CABINET SHUFFLE...

SHUFFLE
SHUFFLE

...A WHOLE NEW LOOK...

19　　　　　　　The Buskers festival coincides with the provincial election.

Service charges.

30

33

THE
FEDERAL GOV'T
PRESENTS

HONEY, I
SHRUNK
THE QUOTAS
(AGAIN)

STARRING: TOM SIDDON
IN HIS ONGOING COMIC ROLE

Bishop Colin Campbell of Antigonish suggests sexual assaults at Mount Cashel may have been partly the victims' fault.

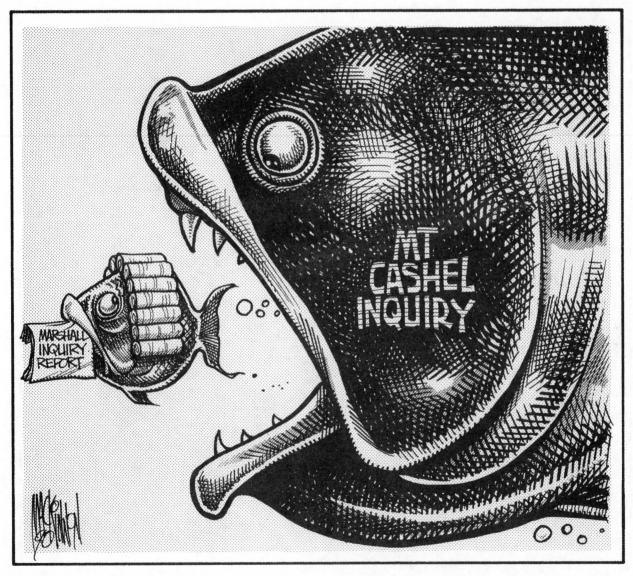

Judge T. Alex Hickman, of the Marshall Inquiry, is implicated in the Mount Cashel scandal.

44

Premier John Buchanan tries to reword his damaging statement suggesting that Nova Scotia join the United States if Meech fails.

STONE AGE MUTANT NINJA TORY

THE LAST SIX-PACK

Former deputy minister Michael Zareski comes forth with startling revelations of patronage, kickbacks, and corruption directly linked to Premier John Buchanan.

54

55

Budget cuts target dental procedures.

National

58

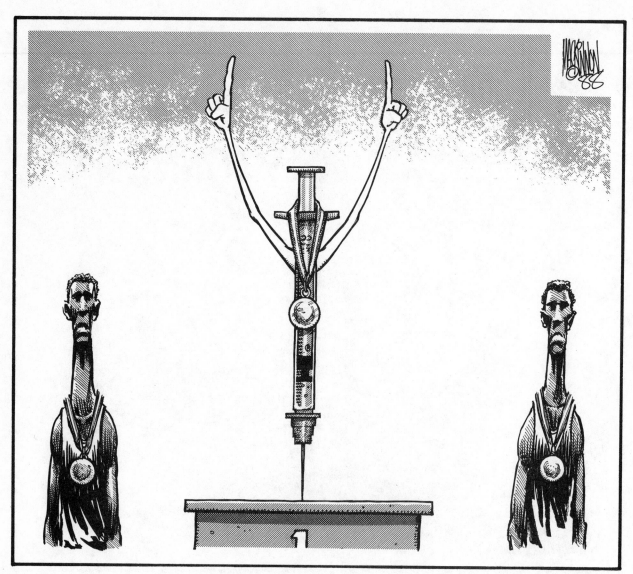

Ben Johnson tests positive for steroids.

70   Ed Broadbent steps down; John Turner remains.

John Turner steps down.

74

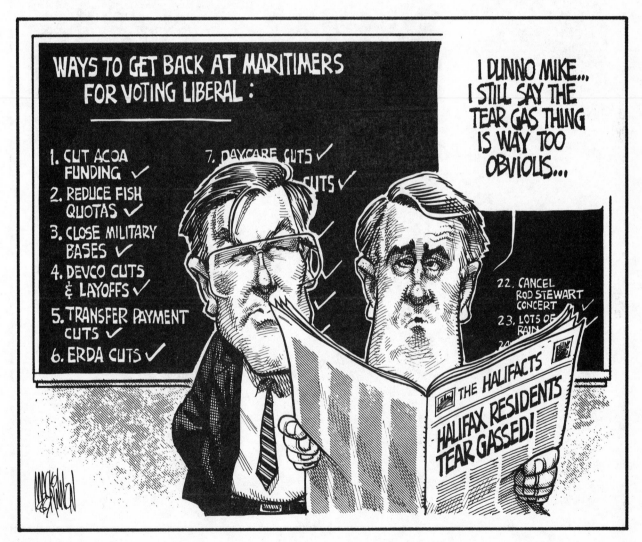

76

Jean Charest

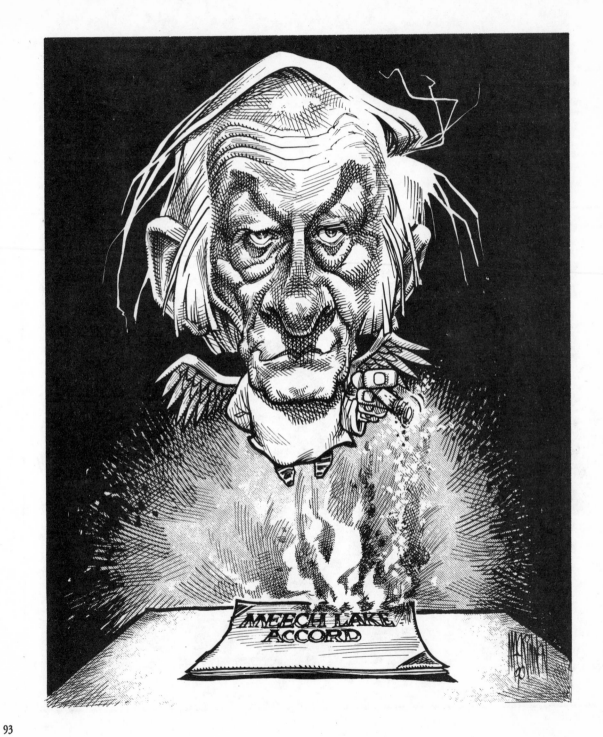

Liberal leadership convention opens with Turner send-off.

International

CLASS OF '89

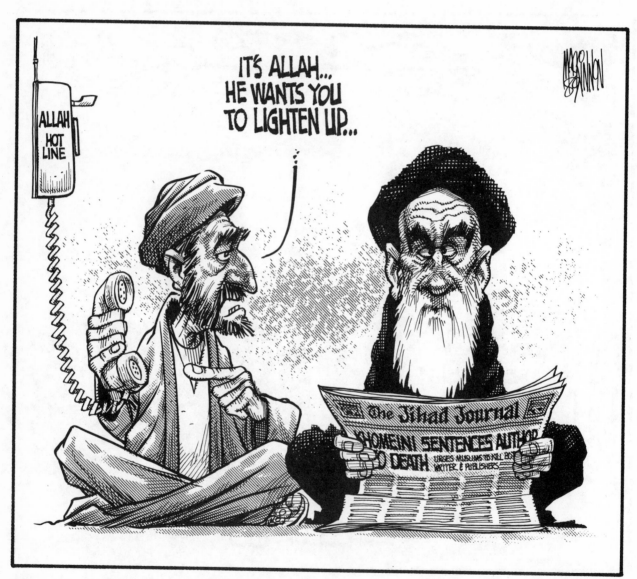

COMMONWEALTH ROWING TEAM

116

117